The Every Day Coin Collector Series:

Introduction
to
Coin Collecting

Darren Kirby

OTHER WRITINGS BY DARREN KIRBY

~Nonfiction~

Pie Iron Recipes
Dutch Oven Recipes
Tin Foil Recipes
The Best Tent Camping Guide

~Novels~

Coordinates For Murder

~Short Story Collections~

Sometimes They Scream

~Short Stories~

Pins and Dolls
The Ritual
f r e q u e n c y
Two Inches of Revenge
A Push Too Far

TABLE OF CONTENTS

INTERNATIONAL DISCLAIMER

This book was written by an American with an American perspective. It was intended primarily for an American audience, so when I generically refer to coins, I'm referring to U.S. Coins.

Those of you who are reading this and are outside the U.S., you can still take away a lot of information in this book and series. Much of what I talk about in this book applies no matter where you are in the world, so don't think that this book isn't for you. Just know that this book is U.S.-centric in its approach.

Happy Collecting!

EVERY DAY COIN COLLECTOR

What Is The Every Day Coin Collector?

The Every Day Coin Collector is a coin collector who chooses to collect coins and notes because they find them interesting. They aren't necessarily out to find really old coins or notes, or to have a collection of coins and notes from every country, or to have a collection that is an investment.

As an Every Day Coin Collector, you want to collect coins and notes that have a personal connection or meaning to you. Perhaps you have a family history where some of your ancestors lived in England, so you are interested to learn and collect coins from the United Kingdom. Or maybe the different animals on the coins of Australia speak to you. Whatever the reason, you enjoy collecting coins and notes that YOU find interesting, and not that someone else tells you that you SHOULD be collecting.

An Every Day Coin Collector isn't always

concerned about what they pay for a coin or note, but you also don't want to overpay or be taken advantage of. An Every Day Coin Collector likes to learn about the hobby and wants to help others get interested in the hobby as well. We aren't flashy, we know what we like, and we're perfectly happy if we are the only ones that enjoy what we collect – because we do it for US!

INTRODUCTION

While this book is titled "Introduction to Coin Collecting", I really cover both coins and bills or notes in this book. The reason for this is because they are naturally related to each other, both being currency, and because typically if you collect one, you also collect the other. For sure most collectors tend toward either coins or notes, but there are some collectors, myself included, that collect both equally. Since this volume covers both coins and notes, why didn't I include the word "notes" in the title? Mostly because of economies of space. There is only so much room on the cover and I didn't want to have a wall of text on the cover. Additionally, most people start collecting coins versus notes because collecting pennies is MUCH more affordable than collecting $10 notes. So, while coins is featured on the cover, this volume will include information on collecting notes as well. And there are some very fun and interesting $1 notes that can be found, so you don't have to look toward the higher denominations right away.

For those of us who enjoy the hobby of

collecting coins and notes, we can all probably point back to at least one incident in our youth that caused us to become enamored with them. For me, I think there were two such incidents. The first was when my family took a trip (and actually did several trips over my formative years) into Canada. Along with being fascinated (and a little frightened) with crossing the border and watching my father interact with the Canadian border guards, I was also fascinated that this other world had their own currency. It looked a lot like the money that I was familiar with in the United States – they had the same denominations in their coins and notes – but yet the imagery and some of the language was very different. Their notes had both English and French written on them, and the person portrayed on the Canadian $1 dollar bill I didn't recognize at the time. But they had some color in them, when I was used to shades of green with the U.S. dollars. This was when I was perhaps 9 or 10 years old.

The other incident came after my parents returned from a cruise in the Carribbean. As part of their trip they stopped in the Bahamas to shop. When they returned they still had some money from the Bahamas, and it was so cool to see how different another countries coins could be. The penny was still copper but had a starfish on one side. But the thing that really astounded me, and that I distinctly remember tucking away to keep forever was a note from the Bahamas. It was a half-dollar note, what would commonly be referred to as a fractional note, which I had never seen before. On one side was dull, single-color designs, but when I turned the note over, all of these bright colors greeted me. Yellows, browns, greens, blues, all of these were colors I had never thought possible on a note, and I wondered why our money was so blah compared to this bright and colorful note.

Those two incidents solidified my interest in collecting coins and notes, and especially looking at currency from around the world. I still have those notes and coins from Canadian and the Bahamas in my collection as well. So that's been what has driven the growth in my collection – finding ways to acquire coins and notes from all over the world, and from any time period. I still enjoy collecting coins and notes from the United States as well because they are easy to come by and provide some interesting history of the country. There is no right or wrong answer to where you start your collection, except that it needs to be interesting to you.

GETTING STARTED

So, where do you get started on collecting coins? Well, most folks will suggest you start with the change you have in your pockets, and there are good reasons for this. First, you probably have quite a bit of change at home that you can pull together and start your collection with. Second, it's pretty easy to get more change as you live your life, buying things and getting change. Third, its a cheap way to get started because you aren't spending big dollars on a single specimen. So, starting with the change you already have is a perfect way to get started.

Once you start combing through your change, you'll quickly find holes that you don't have coins to fill. If you wanted to collect pennies all the way back to 1900, you'll be spending a LOT of time looking through change to find them all, but it still is possible to do it. Same with the rest of the coin denominations. Now you have a new question to ask yourself: what coins do you want to collect?

And the answer here is actually several answers.

For example, with quarters you have the option to start collecting the National Parks, which are the most recent set of quarters and will finish up in 2020. Prior to the National Parks quarters, there was the Statehood Quarters where there was a quarter designed for each state and several U.S. Territories. Prior to these you had more generic quarters, including a special set of coins that celebrated the bicentennial of the United States (the set included a quarter, half-dollar and dollar coins). Or perhaps you want to go further back in history, starting in 1964 and earlier. These quarters have 90% silver content, so these are typically horded for their silver content (as opposed to just outright buying silver for investment) and as such are hard to find in circulation generally.

As you can see, there are many directions that you can go in with your collection. What many people do is to start collecting all of the years of each coin denomination by sorting through their own change. As you do this you may find some odd coins that end up being error coins. These coins are valuable because they basically are accidents that made it through the process and were still issued. Often times you'll find things like a double-strike coin or a coin that is slightly off center. There are literally hundreds of variations of error coins, with some being more common and others being literally one-of-a-kind.

Notes have their own interesting ways of being collected. A regular set of United States notes currently include the one, two, five, ten, twenty, fifty and one hundred dollar bills. These are all notes that are still produced and used by the general public. The two dollar bill is a bit of an anomoly and sometimes causes discussions at retailers who are unfamiliar with them. They are also often given as gifts with birthday cards and such because they are more unique and you rarely see them used as currency. With these notes, you will find that notes do not have the year that they were printed on them like coins, but the year that the particular design was issued. Because the Secretary of the Treasury and the United States Treasurer both feature their signatures on the bills, and the people in these positions changes frequently, new bill designs are issued when these people change. Thus, you will only see a year on a U.S. note when one or both of these people change.

What you get started with is up to you, and you don't have to stay on that track. Perhaps you'll start collecting nickels by going through your change, and finding the different mint marks for each year that they were produced. After a while, you might start to do the same with the other coins. Then, you may change to focus on the dollar coins, collecting all of the presidential dollar coins. The nice part about collecting is that you can go after whatever you like, whenever you like, no matter if it's found in pocket change or you want rare, graded specimens. You collect what you are interested in and enjoy it, that's how you stick with the hobby for the long term.

EQUIPMENT

One of the great aspects of beginning to collect coins is that you really don't need any equipment to start your own collection. However, there are a number of items that you might find you would like to help enjoy your collection even more, and can help in identifying features on coins that are difficult to discern. None of these are terribly expensive, but of course the fancier you get the more expensive they are.

Magnifying Glass - Having a magnifying glass can be a real advantage to better seeing small details on coins and notes. When viewing smaller coins and trying to read the mint year or even the mint mark to know where it was minted, having something to magnify the coin a bit is generally appreciated by most people. Regular magnifying glasses can be easily found in many different stores, and typically magnify from 2 times to 4 times. A cousin item to the magnifying glass is the magnifying bookmark. These are typically made from plastic and magnify 2 times. They are used for reading books and double as a book mark for the book. These are sometimes nice to have when using on notes as they cover a much larger area for magnification.

Jewelers Loupe - Often times you will be wishing your magnifier was more powerful. The jewelers loupe is what you need. These provide more powerful magnification, usually starting at 5 or 10 times magnification and going up from there. With a jewelers loupe you will be able to ensure you can read dates, mint marks, initials and more.

Towel/Pad - When you are dealing with coins, it is best to work with them on materials that won't add any unnecessary dings, dents or scratches. Having a small soft cloth to lay on your desk or table will help with this, and can also provide some good contrasting background to help things stand out on your coin or note.

Cotton Gloves - Normally when you are handling coins, it is best to hold them by the edge so you don't get any oils or grime on the faces of the coin. A great way to counter the oils would be to use soft cotton gloves that will keep your oils off the coins. I would say that when you are handling change and just looking at and for coins that aren't special ones, gloves aren't needed, but still take care in handling them. Once you start to have more valuable coins, gloves make sense to help preserve their value. The same goes for notes, the general notes you find in change you should try not to handle too much, but once you get more valuable notes, gloves will help to preserve their value.

Magnifying Light - Often when you are trying to look at your coins and notes under a magnifying glass, the amount of light you have available just isn't enough. A very nice solution is using a magnifying light. This is a round light that surrounds a magnifying glass, and this is mounted to a moveable arm that is attached to your desk. This allows for hands-free operation of both a strong lighting source as well as the magnification piece, and you can quickly scan coins and notes for imperfections, mint marks, security features and more.

USB Microscope - Technology is such that we now have USB microscopes that allow us to easily magnify our coins and bills and see details on our computer screens. While these aren't terribly expensive, they are a bit more expensive piece of equipment to add to your hobby. Along with the greater magnification offered versus a jewelers loupe, you have the ability to take pictures of these close-up details to share with friends and other hobbyists. These pictures could also be included with your special note or coin to help showcase the detail to others in your albums.

Coin/Note Log - As you acquire coins and notes for your collection, you will want to have a log somewhere that you record what you have in your collection. This will become important when you go to coin or note shows, dealers or other places where you may want to purchase a coin or note. You can quickly search your log to see if you have the item in question and prevent duplicate buying. This can also be useful for identifying holes in your collection so that you can be on the lookout for those missing items. Lastly, you can also see if your coins and notes are appreciating in value if you record what you purchased them for, and you have a basis for pricing them if you decide to sell them.

STORING YOUR
COINS AND NOTES

Once you start building your collection, you'll quickly find that you need a way to organize and store all of the different coins and bills that you'll accumulate. There are many different options, and most likely you'll end up using a combination of these options for your collection.

Cardboard Albums - Probably the first organization tool that you'll end up with for your collection is a cardboard album. These are available for the different denominations, and often there will be several albums that span many years for a particular coin, such as the one cent coin. The coins are difficult to pop into the openings, but this tight fit means that you won't have to worry about coins getting loose and falling out. Plus, because the coins fit so snuggly into the open spots, you can shelve the coin books like you would a regular book on a bookshelf. This provides you with more room for your collection. However, not all coins should go into a coin book like these. There are other options that you may want to consider for your more special coins.

Coin Flips - When you start to have multiples of coins (and it will happen much sooner than you think) you'll want to have a way to store and display the nicer ones in your collection. The plastic coin flip is a great way to accomplish this, and provides a way to add some information about the coin as well. Flips have a couple of pockets, one for the coin and one of a small piece of paper that you can add details to about the coin. Typically these are 2 inches on each side, but you can find smaller and larger sizes for smaller/larger coins. These are handy because they allow easy access to the coin so you can pull it out and examine it with a magnifying glass, etc. One thing to watch out for is flips made with PVC. They might seem nice because they are more flexible, but they can cause irreversible damage to your coin from the chemicals. Try to find the stiffer variety of flips to avoid this, but also take care to not damage the coin by scraping it against rough edges.

2X2s - These are similar to flips but are a bit more permanent. They are typically cardboard squares with plastic covering round holes so that you can see the coin in the middle. They come as rectangles that fold over itself to form a square, and they are usually stapled shut to hold the coin inside. Often times people write on the cardboard about what the coin is so that it can be easily identified. Some drawbacks to this option is that you can't easily take the coin out of the cardboard without basically destroying the cardboard. Additionally, it isn't easy to really view the coin through the plastic, so you don't get a good idea of the condition of the coin. True, many collectors will provide their take on the condition of the coin by using the various coin grading designations, but that's only an opinion and you will want to examine the coin yourself outside of the cardboard holder if you are serious about buying the coin. Additionally, with these 2x2s, you can find plastic binder sheets that will hold these cardboard holders so you can quickly catalog and look through your collection. Alternatively, you can find long boxes that fit these 2x2s so you can store them easily.

Coin Capsules - Sometimes you will have some coins that you would like to easily show off to people and not worry about them handling it and getting oils on the coin. Coin capsules are the way to go in this case. If you can get ones that have foam cut outs to ensure a snug fit, that is even better. These capsules can also open back up again if you need to access the coin at a later date.

Coin Tubes - When you have a lot of a certain type of coin, sometimes coin tubes are the way to go. For example, you might collect every wheat penny that you can find, and instead of putting them all in flips or 2x2s, its easiest to store them in a coin tube. Same with pre-1965 quarters that contain silver, its easiest to store them in coin tubes as you want them for the silver content, not necessarily because they are a high value specimen. These tubes typically hold around 20 to 25 coins each, and can be written on with a Sharpie pen or something similar, so you can quickly identify which coin tube holds what.

Currency Sleeves - This is a great option for showcasing your different currency notes while being able to easily show people. Typically these sleeves are top loading, meaning it is easy to put the notes into the sleeve. These sleeves come in different sizes so you can have the right size for larger bills, regular sized bills and even smaller bills. These work for any currency notes from anywhere in the world.

Currency Note Album - These albums allow you to keep all of your currency notes in one place. Once your note collection gets large enough, an album is a great way to house all of your notes in a single place. These again come in different sizes so you can have all of your large notes in one album and your smaller sized notes in another album. Several different companies offer note albums. In addition, like for coins, you can get multinote sleeves that will fit a standard 3-ring binder and hold up to 4 notes per page for standard size bills, or 3 notes for larger size bills.

Acryllic Picture Holder - You can find picture holders that are clear acryllic that make it appear as your picture is floating in the middle. These make great holders to display your favorite notes, and they allow you to see both sides of the note and to allow others to handle the holder without putting oils on the note.

TECHNOLOGY IN COIN AND NOTE COLLECTING

In our ever expanding digital age, coin and note collecting is notably analog. The hobby is inherently tactile, visceral, real. And perhaps that is why it has been enjoying a resurgence in popularity, because it goes against so much of what we have in our society. And yet, even though numismatics is a physical hobby, there are ways that technology and the digital world can provide us with better information, faster access to resources, and new ways to enjoy and share the hobby with others. These are tools that nearly anyone can have access to and use, and perhaps the frustrating part is just how to use them to benefit us as Every Day Coin Collectors.

Coinoscope App - This is an app for both Android and Apple devices. It is surprising how many people do not know about this app and what it can do yet, but that will change as word spreads. The app utilizes the camera that is built in to your phone to take a picture of a coin. Once the picture is taken, the app searches the Internet for similar pictures and provides a list of results for what it thinks are appropriate websites related to the coin. Now, not all of the search results will apply, but a number of them will, and this is especially useful when trying to determine the country of origin of a coin you are unfamiliar with. Often foreign coins have markings or languages that you cannot decipher, and this app helps. This app is a must-have if you collect foreign coins. Bonus: its free!

Cataloging App - While we know about the importance of having a catalog of the coins and notes that we own, it is not always convenient to carry a book around with us having all of our coins listed. Enter cataloging apps, of which there are several for both coins and notes. This is a way for you to have your current inventory listed in a convenient place: right on your phone. Try out different apps to see which one works best for you. Great when you are at coin shows, flea markets and other places where having access to what you already own is a priority.

Facebook - This might seem a bit odd, listing Facebook as a digital part of coin collecting. However, if you skip Facebook you will be missing thousands of your hobbyist friends that are sharing advice, posting pictures with questions, and generally making the education of coin collecting much more interesting. There are hundreds of coin and note collecting groups around the world, catering to nearly any aspect of the hobby that you might be interested in. Do not overlook this great, free resource.

Instagram - Like Facebook, Instagram is another social media platform that can offer an unending supply of visual representations of many of the worlds most interesting and desirable coins and notes. There are countless people to follow on

Instagram who post photos of the coins and notes that they encounter. Just like Facebook, Instagram is another free resource worth looking into.

YouTube - If a picture is worth a thousand words, coin and note videos are worth far more. Here you will find videos of people doing coin roll hunting, showing off some of their personal collections, and even educational videos from around the world about different country's coins and notes and what makes them so special. The amount of information available to numismatists is staggering, and like the other website above, it is all free.

Blogs - These are fascinating places to check out. From well-known collectors to total unknowns, blogs about coin and note collecting can provide you additional information as well as personal takes on the hobby. Here again these are free resources and provide you with one person's perspective on the hobby of numismatics.

WHERE TO FIND
COINS AND NOTES

There are many ways to build your collection of coins and bills. I'll describe several of them here, but there are many more ways to go about adding to your collection. And there is no "right" way to add to your collection, except the ways that work for you in acquiring the coins and bills that you desire. Try one or several of these options and see if they work for you.

Searching Pocket Change - this is perhaps the easiest and most readily available source of a variety of coins anyone has access to. Any change you have in your pockets or purse at the end of the day goes into a jar. After a week or two, you can spend some time going through all of this change. What you look for depends on your goals, but it might be to look for a particular year to complete your penny collection of Lincoln cents. Or it could be to look for quarters with silver content (1964 and earlier). Whatever your goals, searching your change is a great way to start or add to your collection.

Searching Bills - doing this is the same as searching your change, but typically is faster as you have less bills than you do coins. Regularly search through the bills in your wallet or purse to look for ones that are unusual or are worth adding to your collection. You might be looking to complete your set of $1 bills from a particular year from all 12 regional banks. Or you might be looking for star notes, or even silver certificates. Whatever you look for, checking your bills regularly provides you the option to find these specimens "in the wild" and they might even be in great condition.

Coin Roll Hunting - this method of coin searching involves getting full rolls of coins, usually from banks or credit unions, and searching through the coins in the entire roll looking for special coins for your collection. This has been a popular way to acquire coins for your collection, and sometimes provides special coins that have made their way into circulation. People have found older coins, like Indian head pennies in rolls, or even steel pennies from 1943, or unique error coins. All of these can be found in addition to coins to complete various collections that you have. Other coins offer their own specials: old Mercury head dimes, 40% silver quarters, Buffalo nickels and more. Even half dollar coins have modern specials that can be found: NIFC coins (Not Intended For Circulation). These are coins dated 2002 or later that were minted but only made available by special request; they were never put into general circulation, but somehow have ended up in circulation. You can try your hand at these by picking up a few rolls from your bank, but some people order boxes of rolls at a time to do hardcore searching.

Bank Strap Hunting - this is similar to searching coin rolls, only you are searching bundles of bank bills. This isn't as popular as coin roll hunting, but it can still yield results for your collection. Perhaps one of the reasons bank strap hunting isn't as popular is that at a minimum, you would need to pony up $100 dollars for a strap of $1 dollar bills (there are 100 bills in a strap). Conversely, if you wanted a box of pennies (50 rolls per box), you would only need to put up $25. Not only that, but a box of pennies has 2,500 pennies in total versus only 100 $1 bills in a strap. The odds that you will find something worthwhile is higher in that box of pennies than in a strap of $1 bills. Yet, bank strap hunting might be something to try. You could find silver certificates, star notes, radar notes, low number notes and more.

Metal Detecting - its interesting that one hobby can help with another hobby. If you are into metal detecting, you already know that old coins are a common find when hunting. And while they will never have the luster of an uncirculated coin, the fact that you are digging up history is fun in itself. Why was the coin where you found it? How did the coin get lost? What happened in the area that you found the coin? Lots of questions, many of which don't have answers, but you have the joy of finding a lost piece of history AND of expanding your collection of coins. Consider metal detecting as a new hobby that helps feed your coin collecting hobby.

Garage Sales and Flea Markets - this is not something that I think most collectors think of. Garage sales might feature someone wanting to get rid of their coin collection for a variety of reasons. But just because a garage sale doesn't have any coins or bills out on display doesn't mean the people don't have old coins they would like to get rid of. It pays to ask the person putting on the garage sale or flea market to see if they have any old coins or notes, or even foreign change or bills that they don't want anymore. Many times they just don't think about the coins and notes that they have, but when you ask about it they will be more than happy to talk with you and show you what they have. Maybe they would even consider selling some of them, and you wouldn't have to worry about dealer markups or show "specials" where you end up paying more than you should.

Asking Family and Friends - this is a technique that I have used often when I know people are traveling outside of the country. I think this works best for foreign currency, but it could also be a way to make connections to people who also collect, and you might get new sources for domestic coins and bills as well. By asking people who have traveled overseas, I have gotten foreign money from a variety of different countries that I may never travel to myself. Often they will be good with simply you paying them the exchange rate for the currency, as you are giving them more than they would get at a currency exchange office who charges a fee. The downside to this is that you will most often be getting only modern coins and notes versus older coins and notes, but this to me is a minor downside because there are so many countries to get currency from that even modern currency has thousands of varieties in their notes and coins, so there is a lot to admire and learn about them.

Coin Shows - attending a coin show is a great way to see a LOT of currency in a short amount of time. Plus, you can spend some time talking with other collectors and sharing information, learning what they specialize in, and hopefully making some good connections for later help in completing part of your collection. You can also purchase coins and notes at shows, but it helps greatly to know what something is worth. This is where understanding the coin and bill grading scale really helps out, and being able to judge if you agree with the grades listed on the coins and notes displayed. You may be able to get a good deal at a show, but a good deal is one where both the seller and buyer are both satisfied with the transaction.

Coin Dealer - this is a worthwhile option to help find those rare coins and notes that you are looking for. The one thing that dealers have is a network to tap into to help you find these things. Yes, you will likely pay a premium to get that special coin, but it you try to find it on your own you may be waiting months, even years to get what you are wanting. A coin dealer might be able to locate it within hours or days, but certainly much faster than you can on your own. Not only that, but they are great sources for learning more, understanding how to protect your collection, providing evaluations on some of the pieces in your collection, and more. Don't overlook a dealer just because you might pay more because they offer much more.

ERROR COINS

Millions and millions of coins are struck every year, so it makes sense that some errors during the minting process are bound to occur. Many are caught and the coins never make it into circulation, but that still leaves some that do make it through the process. These error coins command a premium over their normal counterparts because they are inherently rare. Some errors are very minor and unless you were specifically looking for them, you would miss them. However, some errors are very glaring and you know right away that you have an error coin on your hands. Here is a list of some of the errors that you might encounter as you look through your coins, but there are many other errors that may occur.

Off-Center - An off-center mint error can range from slightly off-center to nearly off the planchets. Typically the more off-center a coin is, the more it is worth.

Blank Planchets - These mint errors are incredibly common, and cents can be purchased for just a few dollars.

Die Breaks - Die breaks are very common on early coinage and usually do not bring a premium.

Cuds - These are caused when a portion of the die breaks off, and part of the design is obscured.

Missing Letters - Missing letters are usually caused by grease or foreign material on the dies.

Clipped Planchets - With clipped planchets, the planchets are punched out incorrectly, and portions of the design are missing. These are very common.

Wrong Planchet Errors or Denomination Errors - These errors occur when the wrong planchet from one coin is fed into a press designed for another denomination. Examples of this include a nickel struck on a planchet for dimes. The error coin that is struck on the wrong blank will bear the same weight as the coin that should have been struck correctly.

Double Struck Coins - After the planchet is struck by the die, the feeders eject the coin out of the collar. If the coin is not ejected, it can receive a second, or even more, strike. As a result, you will see multiple designs on the obverse and reverse.

Lamination Flaw - A lamination flaw is a planchet defect that results from metal impurities or internal stresses. Lamination flaws cause discoloration, uneven surfaces, peeling, and splitting.

ERROR NOTES

Like coins, notes can have errors as well. Many errors are caught, and those error notes are replaced right at the mint. We know this because of a thing called Star Notes. A star note is a note that has the last character in the notes unique serial number as an asterisk instead of a letter. While star notes are common, they are obviously less common than normal notes, though many people enjoy collecting star notes since they are unique and different. But there are still many other error notes that do make it into circulation, and these are sought after by collectors and others. As you look through your notes periodically, look for some of these errors to add to your collection.

Shift Errors - These occur when a printing of the note doesn't align with the note's other two printings. These are some of the most commonly encountered errors.

Offset Errors - These are fairly common and happen when wet sheets touch each other leaving imprints of other notes on them.

Extra/Under Inking - These are very noticeable errors but generally don't carry a huge premium. Certain parts (usually the black printed portions) will be too light or too dark, thus classifying them as errors.

Mismatched Serial Numbers - This is fairly self-explanatory; they occur when a note has two different serial numbers.

Fold-Over Errors - When a note is folded improperly when printed, strange parts of the notes get inked that shouldn't. These often affect corners and can lead to serial numbers being on the reverse of the note.

Missing/Misplaced Prints - Notes are printed in three processes. This means that workers have to do several things correctly three times to print the note as we are used to seeing it. Sometimes they miss or mess up a step. This results in black seal or green seal and serials being out of place or completely missing.

Reverse Overprints - Back overprint errors are the result of an uncut sheet being fed into a press with the obverse of the note facing the overprinting press. The information printed by the overprinting press include Treasury and Federal Reserve District seals, district numbers and serial numbers. Such a note will be missing these elements from the front, and instead have each displayed on the back.

Inverted Overprint - When a sheet is fed upside down relative to the existing face print, the result is the Treasury Seal, District Seal, District Number and serial numbers being printed upside down. Inverted 3rd print errors are not especially rare.

Misaligned Overprints - When overprints (3rd printing) occur when the serial numbers and seals are out of position, vertically or horizontally, and are so far from their appropriate position that they cover unintended portions of the note. For example, a District seal might be so far misaligned that it covers the portrait on the face of the note. Again, errors range from minor, to major, with major errors being more desirable to collectors.

Missing 2nd Printing - Similar to Missing Overprints, a note with a missing 2nd print is recognizable because the note is missing its face printing. Therefore no subject or denomination is displayed on the note.

Inverted Errors - These errors often go unnoticed because you have to bend the note to see both sides at once to identify them. For an inverted error to exist the front would be normal and the back upside down, or vice versa.

Cutting Errors - Cutting errors are some of the most noticeable and most valuable of errors. These happen when a sheet of notes is skewed when it is cut. This can lead to extra parts and strange looking additions.

Gutter Fold or Blank Crease - Gutter folds are the result of the uncut sheets being sent through the press with a wrinkle or wrinkles in the paper. A gutter fold error note may have one wrinkle or multiple wrinkles. While collectible, these errors are relatively common.

Ink Smears - As the name implies, an ink smear error occurs when smears of ink are passed from the press onto a note. Ink smears are not hard to duplicate or fake, so be wary when purchasing.

Obstruction Errors - As the name suggests, during the printing something physically got in the way of the note causing the note to be blank where the obstruction was.   These have even more value if the note still has the obstruction attached.

Double Denomination Errors - These are the kings of errors and the most valuable. They happen when a note is printed with one denomination on the front and different one on the bank. They rarely happen and are worth a lot of money.

UNDERSTANDING THE
COIN GRADING SYSTEM

The coin grading system is one that you'll want to get familiar with, as nearly everyone uses this grading system. However, the system itself is a bit subjective, even though the grading companies have a number of points that would help to "lock in" a particular grade level. The grading companies can be fairly well trusted to have consistent grading, but when you go to independent collectors and dealers, when they grade their own coins, it can be a bit more subjective. As such, its good to understand the grading system so that you can make your own determination on a coin, and perhaps you can work a price for a coin down by pointing out issues, or you might find a deal on a coin that is graded lower than you feel it should be.

So, what is the grading system? The system is referred to as the Sheldon Coin Grading Scale, and was developed in 1949 by Dr. William Sheldon. He developed a grading scale from 1 to 70, with 1 being very poor quality and 70 being nearly flawless and uncirculated. Beginning in the 1970s, this scale was refined more to provide a greater variety of rankings, especially when you get to scoring from MS60 to MS70. The scale that I've listed in this book is the general rankings that the major coin grading companies use, along with some descriptions for each level.

As you look at more and more coins, especially those that are professionally graded, and even some privately graded coins from reputable collectors/dealers, you will start to get a feel for what a coin would grade at. Based on this grading, along with other factors, a coin will be worth more or less. Most beginning collectors will not need to be concerned with coin grades, but as you learn more you will begin to get interested in the coin grades, and you will likely encounter graded coins at coin shows that you may attend. As you focus on particular coins for your collection, you may be inclined to only look for coins that are graded as AU50 or better. But don't get caught up in the grading system as your only metric for determining what you will pay for a coin, as it is only one part of the story. In the end, as an every day coin collector, you will be collecting coins because of various aspects of enjoyment, and not necessarily seeking a profit from owning and holding onto a coin.

Why Get A Coin Graded

Having a coin graded is not something to take lightly. After all, there is the expense of having it graded, the expense of insuring it during shipping, and then its possible that the grade that comes back won't be what you expect, and could end up costing you more in lost value with a lower grade. However, even with all of these potential negatives and costs, there are still good reasons for having a coin graded.

First, and perhaps most important, is the fact that having a coin professionally graded means that a third-party that is independent from the buyer and seller has given the coin a particular grade, or level of quality. This helps to eliminate disagreements between parties because neither can point to the other as trying to under or over grade the coin. Both parties might agree that the grade given isn't correct, but at least there is an independent grade that they can work from.

Second, having a coin graded today means that it will be encased in a protective slab. This allows people to look at your coin without mishandling it, and it protects it from further damage from accidental handling or dropping. This helps to preserve the coin and hopefully will result in an increase in the price of the coin as time goes on. This is especially important with rare, low mintage and/or high value coins.

Even if you don't have your coins professionally graded, it might be something that you want to learn more about to providing grading on your own. There are several books and videos available to teach you the basics of grading coins. As you get better at it, you will find that you start evaluating others' grades on their coins to see if you would grade it the same or not. The American Numismatic Association offers a correspondence course in coin grading that will enable you to better grade your own coins, as well as to know if other's gradings are accurate.

Lettering explanations:

MS = Mint State
PF = Proof
AU = About Uncirculated
XF = Extremely Fine
VF = Very Fine
F = Fine
VG = Very Good
G = Good
AG = About Good
FR = Fair
PO = Poor

Coin Grading Scale:

MS/PF 70: A coin with no post-production imperfections at 5x magnification

MS/PF 69: A fully struck coin with nearly imperceptible imperfections

MS/PF 68: Very sharply struck with only miniscule imperfections

MS/PF 67: Sharply struck with only a few imperfections

MS/PF 66: Very well struck with minimal marks and hairlines

MS/PF 65: Well struck with moderate marks or hairlines

MS/PF 64: Average or better strike with several obvious marks or hairlines and other miniscule imperfections

MS/PF 63: Slightly weak or average strike with moderate abrasions and hairlines of varying sizes

MS/PF 62: Slightly weak or average strike with no trace of wear. More or larger abrasions than an MS/PF 63

MS/PF 61: Weak or average strike with no trace of wear. More marks and/or multiple large abrasions

MS/PF 60: Weak or average strike with no trace of wear. Numerous abrasions, hairlines and/or large marks

AU 58: Slight wear on the highest points of the design. Full details

AU 55: Slight wear on less than 50% of the design. Full details

AU 53: Slight wear on more than 50% of the design. Full details except for very minor softness on the high points

AU 50: Slight wear on more than 50% of the design. Full details except for minor softness on the high points

XF 45: Complete details with minor wear on some of the high points

XF 40: Complete details with minor wear on most of the high points

VF 35: Complete details with wear on all of the high points

VF 30: Nearly complete details with moderate softness on the design areas

VF 25: Nearly complete details with more softness on the design areas

VF 20: Moderate design detail with sharp letters and digits

F 15: Recessed areas show slight softness. Letters and digits are sharp

F 12: Recessed areas show more softness. Letters and digits are sharp

VG 10: Wear throughout the design. Letters and digits show softness

VG 8: Wear throughout the design. Letters and digits show more softness

G 6: Peripheral letters and digits are full. Rims are sharp

G 4: Peripheral letters and digits are nearly full. Rims exhibit wear

AG 3: Most letters and digits are readable. Rims are worn into the fields

FR 2: Some details are visible. Rims are barely visible

PO 1: Enough detail to identify the coin's date and type. Rims are flat or nearly flat

This grading scale is courtesy NGC website:
www.ngccoin.com/coin-grading/grading-scale/

UNDERSTANDING THE NOTE GRADING SYSTEM

Like the Coin Grading System described earlier, the Note Grading System operates in a similar way using the Sheldon Grading Scale. Like coins, notes have several features that could make them worth more or less, including folds, being off-center, traces of handling, rips/tears and more. The purpose of grading your notes is to establish an agreed upon basis for the quality of the note, and then a price can be negotiated from there. As you get started collecting notes, you will not likely have any that are worth the price of grading. Over time, you will encounter notes that are graded and are ones that you would like to own, and you may even acquire old notes that are in need of grading and preserving. Understanding the grading scale will help in your understanding and appreciation of notes, and what is a fair price for each note. However, like coins, don't let the grading be your sole reason for acquiring a note. You need to know what you want in your collection, and a graded note may not be needed for your collection.

Why Get A Note Graded

The reasons to get a note graded are basically the same as the reasons to get a coin graded: independent grading and protecting the note itself. Independent grading helps to ensure that buyers and sellers have some basis of agreement, allowing for more smooth transactions amongst the collectors. And protecting the note is important so that it survives and doesn't receive any further damage, just like with coins. And, just like when deciding to get a coin graded, having a note graded is not something to be taken lightly.

Note grading hasn't been around as long as coin grading, note grading having only gotten started in 2005 (coin grading has been around for several decades longer). However, its importance for the hobby cannot be underestimated. Unfortunately there is not currently any available courses for grading notes like there is for grading coins, but I'm sure this will change as time goes on. Read books, watch videos and try to work on grading your own notes, and you'll become more adept at grading other notes and to evaluate them carefully before buying them, graded or otherwise.

Note Grading Scale:

70 EPQ: The highest grade assigned. Notes must have no evidence of handling visible at 5x magnification. The margins and registration must appear centered to the unaided eye. Notes must qualify for the PMG Star () Designation to be graded 70

69 EPQ: This note is nearly visually indistinguishable from a 70 but the margins and registration may appear slightly off center. There is no evidence of handling visible to the unaided eye

68 EPQ: The margins and registration are slightly off center. There may be very minor handling

67 EPQ: A note with above-average margins and registration. There may be minor handling

66 EPQ: There may be slightly more handling than a 67 EPQ note. The centering must be above average

65 EPQ: The note may have one or two minor distractions as a result of minor handling. The centering must be above average

64: The centering is off on one or two sides. Some handling may be evident but there must be no folds in the design

63: The centering is imperfect and the design may be flat. There may be several flaws but there will be no folds

62: The note is strictly uncirculated but may have minor-to-moderate handling and/or corner tip issues. There will be no folds, however. The margins may touch or come into the design

61: The note is poorly centered and the margins come into the design. There may be counting marks, smudges or other signs of handling. There will be no folds through the design

60: A note with problems that may include toned paper, a small stain or fading. There will be handling issues but there will be no folds through the design

58: Often a note with a single fold that crosses the design

55: This grade is commonly assigned to a note that has one fold or two to three corner folds through the design

53: A note with two vertical folds or a single horizontal fold. May also have signs of handling

50: The note has two heavier folds or light horizontal and vertical folds. The handling can be significant

45: A note with two to three heavy folds, one of which may be horizontal

40: There are three or more folds, one of which may be horizontal

35: For years dealers and collectors called this grade "VF-XF." This note looks Extremely Fine, but it will have four to seven light folds

30: This note will be lightly circulated and may have light soiling. There will typically be seven to ten folds

25: A note that shows modest evidence of circulation as well as more folds and/or soiling than a note graded 30

20: The note is moderately circulated with numerous folds, mild soiling. There are no serious detractions but there may be minor defects

15: This note may look like a Very Fine note, but upon closer examination it is found to have too many folds or too much circulation to warrant a Very Fine grade

12: The evidence of circulation is considerable with rounded corners, margin splits and other issues. The note must be whole with solid paper
10: A solid, whole note with lots of circulation. The note is too limp and has a number of minor problems

8: The note is heavily circulated but is intact. Some small pieces may be missing. Soiling, light stains or splits are common for this grade. The note is limp
6: The note is very worn with serious splits, fraying of the margins and damage

4: A very heavily circulated note with numerous problems. It is totally limp with impaired visual appeal. Notes in this grade are commonly seen with pieces missing

This grading scale is courtesy PMG website:
www.pmgnotes.com/paper-money-grading/grading-scale/

REFERENCE BOOKS

As with most things in life, there are plenty of books devoted to the subject of coin collecting. You could end up having a side collection of coin collecting books! But in reality, its not a bad idea to consider having at least a few books that you use as reference books for your collection. Here are a few that you may want to invest in.

Every Day Coin Collector Books - This series of books is designed to provide you with quick reference to coin collecting in general as well as specific sets of coins, such as the Statehood Quarters or the Presidential Dollar Coins. An ever-expanding series that will be referred to frequently because of the ability for fast reference and solid information.

The Official Red Book - This is the book that most collectors refer to when they need to know mintages of certain coins, it provides you with some possible pricing for your coin based on various grades, shows some of the more common errors on a variety of coins and more. This is an annual publication, and while most information doesn't change, every year provides new coins that are minted, errors discovered, etc. Having a copy of this book on your shelf should be a high priority for research.

The Official Blue Book - This is the companion book to The Official Red Book. The difference with this book is that it is geared for dealers, and provides pricing for what dealers often pay for certain coins. Where the Red Book is for the general public for information and possible pricing, the Blue Book is for the dealer and serious collector looking to know what their collection should be worth.

A Guide Book of United States Paper Money - This is the book to help you understand American currency notes, how many of them were produced, and what their value may be. The book also provides details about the Friedberg numbering system for cataloging your notes as well as error notes, fractional currency and more.

Coin Collecting for Dummies - Part of the "for Dummies" line of books, this volume provides a good reference for how to get started in collecting coins. Its good because it covers a lot of ground, but it is more than 10 years old now and there has been a whole new set of U.S. Quarters that is not covered in this book (plus other denominations).

Whitman Guide to Coin Collecting - Written by a former president of the American Numismatic Association (ANA), this book covers a lot of ground. From how to get started in the hobby to how to care for a collection, with full explanations of grading techniques and standards, coin prices, and values, this book addresses everything clearly and with easy-to-follow detail.

TERMINOLOGY

Like any speciality, numismatics has its own set of special words and definitions that are helpful to know when talking with other coin and note collectors. If you don't know what the obverse of a coin is, or what reeding is, or if you aren't sure what a gold certificate is, then this list of terms is a great place to start learning. This isn't fully comprehensive but will give you a solid base to understanding the peculiar words used in the world of coin and note collecting. Don't worry if you don't remember all of these terms right away, the more you talk with other coin and note collectors, the more these terms will become part of your vocabulary. Because coins and notes have different features, different errors and are made in different ways, each deserves their own set of definitions to better understand and appreciate them. We'll cover terms used for coins first, then cover terms used for notes second.

Common Coin Terms

Alloy - A mixture of two or more metals

American Numismatic Association (ANA) - Nonprofit educational organization that encourages the study of money throughout the world

Annealing - Heating blanks (planchets) in a furnace that softens the metal

Assay - To analyze and determine the purity of metal

Bag Mark - A mark on a coin from contact with other coins in a mint bag

Bi-Metallic - A coin comprised of two different metals, bonded together

Blank - Another word for planchet, the blank piece of metal on which a coin design is stamped

Bullion - Platinum, gold or silver in the form of bars or other storage shapes, including coins and ingots

Bullion Coin - Precious metal coin traded at current bullion prices

Business Strike - A coin produced for general circulation (as opposed to a proof or uncirculated coin specially made for collectors)

Bust - A portrait on a coin, usually including the head, neck and upper shoulders

Clad Coinage - Coins that have a core and outer layer made of different metals. Since 1965, all circulating U.S.

dimes, quarters, half dollars, and dollars have been clad

Coin - Flat piece of metal issued by the government as money

Collar - A metal piece that restrains the expanding metal of a planchet during striking

Commemorative - A special coin or medal issued to honor an outstanding person, place, or event

Condition - The physical state of a coin
Counterfeit - A fake coin or other piece of currency made so that people will think it's genuine

Currency - Any kind of money – coins or paper money – that's used as a medium of exchange

Denomination - The different values of money

Die - An engraved stamp used for impressing a design (images, value, and mottoes) upon a blank piece of metal to make a coin

Designer - The artist who creates a coin's design (but doesn't necessarily engrave the design into a coinage die)

Edge - The outer border of a coin, considered the "third side" (not to be confused with "rim")

Engraver - An artist who sculpts a clay model of a coin's design in bas relief

Error - An improperly produced coin, overlooked in production, and later released into circulation

Face Value - The sum for which a coin can be spent or exchanged (a dime's face value is 10¢) as opposed to its collector or precious metal value

Field - The portion of a coin's surface not used for design or inscription

Grade - Rating which indicates how much a coin has worn from circulation

Hairlines - Tiny lines or scratches on coins, usually caused by cleaning or polishing

Incuse - Opposite of relief, the part of a coin's design that is pressed into the surface

Ingot - Metal cast into a particular shape; used in making coins

Inscription - Words stamped on a coin or medal

Intrinsic Value (Bullion Value) - Current market value of the precious metal in a coin

Key Date - A scarce date required to complete a collection, usually more difficult to find and afford

Legal Tender - Coins, dollar bills or other currency issued by a government as official money

Legend - Principal lettering on a coin

Medal - A metal object resembling a coin issued to recognize an event, place, person or group, with no stated value and not intended to circulate as money

Medium of Exchange - Anything that people agree has a certain value

Mint - A place where coins of a country are manufactured under government authority

Mint Luster - The dull, frosty, or satiny shine found on uncirculated coins

Mint Mark - A small letter on a coin identifying which of the United States Mint's facilities struck the coin

Mint Set - A complete set of coins of each denomination produced by a particular mint
Mint State - Same as uncirculated

Mintage - The quantity of coins produced

Motto - A word, sentence or phrase inscribed on a coin to express a guiding national principle, such as, "E Pluribus Unum" inscribed on all U.S. circulating coins is Latin for "out of many, one"

Mylar® - Trademark for a polyester film used to store coins.

Numismatics - The study and collecting of things that are used as money, including coins, tokens, paper bills, and medals

Obsolete - A coin design or type that is no longer produced

Obverse - The front (or "heads") side of a coin

Off-Center - Describes a coin that has received misaligned strike from the coin press and has portions of its design missing

Overstrike - A new coin produced with a previously struck coin used as the planchet

Pattern - An experimental or trial piece, generally of a new design or metal

Planchet - The blank piece of metal on which a coin design is stamped

Proof - A specially produced coin made from highly polished planchets and dies and often struck more than once to accent the design. Proof coins receive the highest quality strike possible and can be distinguished by their mirror-like background and frosted foreground

Proof Set - A complete set of proof coins of each denomination made in a year

Relief - The part of a coin's design that is raised above the surface, opposite of incuse

Restrike - A coin that is minted using the original dies but at a later date

Reverse - The back (or "tails") side of a coin

Riddler - A machine that screens out blanks (planchets) that are the wrong size or shape

Rim - The raised edge on both sides of a coin (created by the upsetting mill) that helps protect the coin's design from wear

Roll - Coins packaged by banks, dealers or the United States Mint

Series - A collection of coins that contains all date and mint marks of a specific design and denomination

Slab - Nickname for some protective coin encapsulation methods, especially those that are permanently sealed and rectangular

Strike - The process of stamping a coin blank with a design. The strength of the imprint – full, average, or weak – affects the value of rare coins

Type Set - A collection of coins based on denomination

Uncirculated - The term "uncirculated" may have three different meanings when applied to a coin:

1- It can refer to the particular manufacturing process by which a coin is made
2- It can be used as a grade when referring to a coin's degree of preservation and quality of the strike
3- It can point to the fact that a coin has not been used in everyday commerce

At the United States Mint, the term uncirculated refers to the special coining process used to make the coin, which gives it a brilliant finish. Uncirculated coins are manufactured using the same process as circulating coins, but with quality enhancements such as slightly higher coining force, early strikes from dies, special cleaning after stamping, and special packaging. Uncirculated coins may vary to some degree because of blemishes, toning, or slight imperfections.

Upsetting Mill - A machine that raises the rim on both sides of a blank (planchet)

Variety - A minor change from the basic design type of a coin

Year Set - A collection of all coins issued by a country for any one year (does not necessarily include every mint mark)

This terminology list is courtesy U.S. Mint website: www.usmint.gov/collecting-basics/glossary

Common Note Terms

Back - Preferred term for the reverse side of a note

Back Plate Number - Small number found on the lower right side of the back of a bill. Officially known as a Check Number, it provides a cross-reference to the Plate Serial Number on the front

Banknote - Paper currency issued by a bank as opposed to a government

BEP - The Bureau of Engraving and Printing

Border - Outer edge of the design on the back and front where the design ends and plain currency paper begins

Brick - Unit of measurement used by the BEP. A strap is 100 notes banded together, forty straps make a brick. Consists of 4000 notes weighing about 4 kilograms or 8.8 pounds.

Broken Bank Note - Currency issued by a now defunct bank. Also referred to as obsolete banknote

Check Number - Small number found on the lower right of a note, used to cross reference plate numbers

Condition - Grade or state of preservation of paper currency

Continental Currency - Paper money first issued in 1775 by the Continental Congress, originally backed by Spanish milled dollars

Counterfeit - Currency specifically created to look like genuine currency with the intent to defraud

Currency - Legal tender referring usually to paper money, but can be applied to coins and notes

Decimalization - A process of changing the ratio between the main and the subunit of a currency to an integral power of 10. This is not to be confused with Redenomination

Denomination - Face value or amount a coin or note is worth

District Number - The Federal Reserve District Number appears four times on the face of a bill for identification purposes

Engraving - Labor intensive process where the design of a bill is engraved onto a steel printing plate

Error Note - Piece of currency that has a manufacturing mistake or misprint

Face - Preferred term for the front side of paper currency

Federal Reserve District Seal - Found to the left of the portrait on United States currency, it identifies the Federal Reserve Bank that issued the note

Federal Reserve Bank Note - Series of U.S. paper money once authorized by the Federal Reserve, now obsolete. The bank that issued the note was obliged not the Federal Reserve System

Federal Reserve Note - The only form of money now being printed by the United States

Gold Certificate - form of U.S. paper money redeemable for gold coin at one time

Grade - Condition or state of preservation of a piece of paper money

Greenback - Issued in 1861 as a Demand Note. Green Ink used as an anti-counterfeiting measure. Today, almost all US currency is termed "Greenback"

Horse Blanket - Popular term for large size U.S. Notes

Imprint - Name of printer on the note

Large Size - Refers to U.S. paper money that measures 7 3/8 x 3 1/8 inches, issued from 1861 to 1928

Microprinting - Anti-counterfeiting measure where printing within certain areas can be as small as six thousandths of an inch

Prefix - Letter/s over number with numbers following in serial number

Press - High speed machinery on which paper money is printed

Printing Plate - Sheet of steel onto which the note design has been engraved

Radar Note - A banknote in which the serial number reads the same backwards as forwards

Redenomination - The replacement of old currency for newer currency, this usually involves the taking off of some zeroes as years of inflation have reduced the value of the currency. As one example, in 1993 one thousand Mexican pesos were replaced by one Nuevo peso

Replacement Banknote - A note printed with a special symbol before the serial number, or with a special serial number prefix, used to replace notes damaged during the manufacturing process. US replacement notes are called Star Notes because a five pointed star is positioned at the beginning or end of the serial number. Older Canadian replacement notes are known as asterisk notes because an asterisk preceded the serial number. Modern Canadian replacement notes use a special serial number prefix. Italy reserved the letter X as the first letter of the serial number in replacement notes before adopting the euro. Other countries may use different methods

Reserve Bank - Central bank of some countries

Security Thread - Anti-counterfeiting measure of a polymer strip embedded into the currency paper. Usually visible when held to bright light and glows red when held to ultraviolet

Series - Set of years banknote was printed with a specific design and denomination

Serial Number - Identifying number on a note, used to track production and anti-counterfeiting. Serial numbers on US notes are on the face, but other countries' notes can have them on the back or on both sides

Series Date - Notes are dated when they were authorized or first issued. Notes carry that same date throughout their lifespan

Silver Certificate - Certificate of ownership that silver owners hold instead of storing the actual silver

Small Size - Refers to modern U.S. paper currency that measures 6 1/8 x 2 5/8 inches, first issued in 1929

Star Note - See replacement note above

Suffix - Letters that appear after serial numbers (123456ADE)

Syngraphics - Word coined in 1974 to denote the study and collecting of paper money. Based on the Latin word syngrapha, meaning a written promise to pay

Treasury Note - Also known as a coin note, they were first issued in 1890 and redeemable for gold and silver coins

Uniface - Banknote with printing on one side only

Vignette - Picture on a note that fades into the background rather than being framed by a border

Watermark - Embedded anti-counterfeiting design created by varying the density and thickness of the paper. Can be seen when held up to light

This terminology list is courtesy Wikipedia website: https://en.wikipedia.org/wiki/Glossary_of_notaphily

WEBSITE RESOURCES

Of course, books like this one are a great resource for the coin and note collector, but there are a number of valuable websites that can yield a mountain of great information as well. Many of these websites you will want to return to periodically to see what changes are coming along, new mintings, new books, etc. This is by no means an exhaustive list, but merely places to get you started and lead you on to further research and information.

Every Day Coin Collector

www.darrenkirby.com/edcc - This website is the home of all of the Every Day Coin Collector books. Check back regularly to see what new book is being worked on, and check out the author's other books as well.

American Numismatic Association

www.money.org - This organization was formed to advance the knowledge of numismatics, and is dedicated to educating and encouraging people to study and collect coins and related items. Their headquarters is in Colorado Springs, Colorado.

American Numismatic Society

www.numismatics.org - The American Numismatic Society is an organization dedicated to the study of coins, currency, medals, tokens, and related objects from all cultures, past and present. The Society's headquarters in New York City has the foremost research collection and library specialized in numismatics in the United States.

United States Mint

www.usmint.gov - This is the official website for the U.S. Mint. Here you can find details on current coin and note designs, upcoming design releases and more.

Bureau of Engraving and Printing

www.moneyfactory.gov - This is the official website for the Bureau of Engraving & Printing, which produces all of the paper currency for the United States. Here you can find details about the security features on the notes, history of the notes and more

Littleton Coin Company

www.littletoncoin.com - Littleton Coin offers not only supplies for storing and displaying your coins and notes, but also provides some coins and notes for sale as well

Whitman Publishing

www.whitman.com - Whitman Publishing is perhaps best known for their cardboard coin albums, but they also offer many other storage options for coins and notes

Error Reference Website

www.error-ref.com - This website is a comprehensive listing of the different errors in coins, and they are categorized for you as well

Independent Coin Graders

www.icgcoin.com – ICG is a third-party coin grading service. This website provides details about them, the grading process and more

Professional Coin Grading Service

www.pcgs.com – PCGS is a third-party coin grading service that was started in 1986. This website provides details about them, the grading process and more

Numismatic Guaranty Corporation

www.ngccoin.com – NGC is a third-party coin grading service that started in 1987. This website provides details about them, the grading process and more

Paper Money Guaranty

www.pmgnotes.com – PMG is a third-party note grading service that started in 2005. This website provides details about them, the grading process and more

ABOUT THE AUTHOR

Darren is an avid outdoors person, along with his wife. They love to go tent camping all over the north woods of Wisconsin. He also has a love of the written word, having been a writing for more than 10 years. "Introduction to Coin Collecting" is the first in a series of books called the Every Day Coin Collector. He compiled a set of outdoor cookbooks in the Northwoods Cooking Collection that includes "Pie Iron Recipes", "Dutch Oven Recipes" and "Tin Foil Recipes". Additionally, he wrote a tent camping guide for all tent campers from beginner to expert titled "The Best Tent Camping Guide". He is also a novelist, having published "Coordinates For Murder", and has a short story collection titled "Sometimes They Scream". He lives in the north woods of Wisconsin with his beloved wife and two mischievous felines.

www.ingramcontent.com/pod-product-compliance
Lightning Source LLC
Chambersburg PA
CBHW072113150726

47999CB00005B/2013